Published by Sungold Editions

Paperback ISBN-13: 979-8-9910760-1-2

Skipping Across the Surface of Solitude

Poems by
Nathaniel Mayes, Jr.

SUNGOLD EDITIONS • SANTA BARBARA
2024

Dedicated to Nathaniel Mayes, Sr.

*A World War II vet whose undergraduate and graduate
school area of concentration was English Literature,
my father passed away when I was 8 years old.*

CONTENTS

"Music [and poetry are] my refuge.
I could crawl into the space between the notes
[and lines] and curl my back to loneliness."

Adapted from Maya Angelou

DEATH OF A BLACK DAD
DOWN SOUTH...1949

Wailing wind sends
acidic tears scraping
   ...down my cheeks,

my soul sucked shallow.
Love and death
   cymbals clash

from our preacher pitching
reverence for painful gain
   with the holy spirit. Eight,

I feel only hate as I am
left powerless and have
   to swallow poisoned joy.

The choir
screeches off-key as deep
   in southern forests,

my full moon crumbles.
Dad crashes his car
   into the storm of death

with no goodbye.
Mom exhales and we receive
prayerful preacher mumbles,

but I curse Big God,
who, of all beings,
   should know

that a small
Black boy
   needs his dad

when left alone
in Georgia's
   white-faced woods.

SACRED SOUTHERN BLUES

I sat on a small red stool
in my grandma's backyard garden
   with brown snakes, slugs

and skittering bugs,
my grass-stained ankles
   quivering.

I listened to the musical drum riffs
of large frogs croaking in sync
   with the jabbing jig sounds

of worm-beaked crows
aerating earth.
   I tried to see

through soiled windows
of faith. In my dreams
   I'd vanish into the holes

of the universe
created by the Almighty's
   fingernails and I craved

for Grandma
to return from death.
  She'd admonish me

to cut wood and make fire
for Grandpa, as he sat
  with his pipe smoke

that always lifted me
into the ether of hope
  beyond life's clutter

of contradictions.
When Grandpa smiled
  and sang

"Let My People Go" and
"Swing Low, Sweet Chariot,"
  sacred tunes, I crooned along with him.

But these sacred hymns clashed
with the background sounds
  of the blues that came from

the moonshine shack down the street
from the church like when B. B. King was singing
  "Rock Me Baby, Rock Me All Night Long" and

Bessie Smith crooned "I Need A Little Sugar
In My Bowl, I Need A Hot Dog on My Roll,"
   sinful tunes or so the Gospel said.

These "wicked" blues sounds, though,
seemed to fit the carnal scenes
   of Mrs. Wright and Reverend Reynolds

furiously making out on the church's basement
floor after a Saturday night fundraiser
   to expand the space of our holy place.

Nurturing ourselves
within the womb of the church,
   we, the still faithful, prayed

alongside fellow serpents
and swans, colorful colored folks
   all prim and proper with feathered

hats, slicked-down hair,
razor-creased pants and crooked smiles.
   Yes, all sweet souls-for-a-day,

kneeling low, as we made life-and-death
deals with God when the tithing plate
   slid by. Everyone reached down deep

to place their fear-sweat coins in
as a hedge against being left
    at Devil's door before

the coming of the Lord...
because the Bible told us so.
    And down front, as always, I saw

Mrs. Wright screaming out in ecstasy
Can I get a holy hallelujah now?
    ...Sad and confused, I needed to hold tight

to faith, as I almost, but never said,
you mean can you get a down-home,
    sensual and bluesy amen.

ROSE BLOSSOM BLUES

In spring,
   I spring
away from winter,

casting wild
   my petal lures.
I open wide for all

to find me
   yearning
for morning's moisture.

Bedazzled
   by the buzz
of noon's erotic bees,

I hunger for the gaze
   of only those eyes,
that crave carnal rapture.

I pray they see me
   before Sun goes down
when I am left

bereft
   to dream with all of you,
my lonely leaves.

I KNEW SHE WAS A KEEPER
WHEN SHE SAID

I am an unpredictable lady
with an obscure origin

and perverse passions, a lady
who lives raw and revels

in the fervor of musically grooving
underneath a modest-seeming life.

I possess the peculiars that puzzle
the heart and bewitches poets

to float in a sensual sea
of cool metaphors

enough for them to crave deeply
diving down into my mysterious love-lava

that seduces all to succumb to the sway
of my seductive-muse madness.

BOULDER PEBBLE DREAMS

I see you,
a beautiful skipping pebble,
  slim and shiny

as you skim the surface
of my sea. You see me below
  the waves and you're tempted

by engagement with the deep,
for I'm at water's floor, a boulder,
  rough-edged on one side,

but smooth on the other.
I long to be lifted
  to the surface and transformed

by Love's large hands,
so I could be free
  to surf with you

on our smooth sides.
Together we could skip
  across the surface

of solitude, sailing smoothly
on waves, wanting to be
   no more than who we are:

a skipping pebble coupled
with a large boulder,
   showing our best sides

to an astounded world.

VAMPIRES, ZOMBIES AND LOVE

I am sick
of reading so many

    love poems. They're greedy
    mosquitoes seeking

to exact from me
bloodsucking cravings.

No love poems from me.
This is my rant about

    all the metastasized metaphors
    of lasting truths,

of amour. Not a trace of
those rotting seeds

    can grow in me now, as I have
    heartburn from swallowing

love-seared bitter mangoes.
I'm buried in the hardened soil

of apathy, as if I've been bitten
by a Vampire who sucked all warmth

out of me. But like a Zombie on steroids,
those poems and god-damn feelings

insist on rising again and again
within me, and you

make me bellow out
and bow down

with sorrowful melodies
as I pray for you

to return from the grave.
Come back to me you lovely

love-sucking Vamp, so I can rise
to live and fall

in love with love poems
once again.

Dedicated to my deceased wife of 40 years

DON'T COME AROUND MUCH ANYMORE

It was the blaring buzz,
    the stormy swarm of bees
in my dream
    that made me feel

      the stinging loss of you
        in my life
my beautiful goodbye-honeybee.
    You left me,

      a sour lonely Jaguar,
    after gifting me
      with the fragrance
    of your sweet nectar.

Ever since you soared
    around me
 from your spirit world
    as my beautiful apparition

you have reminded me
    that I had forgotten

how to walk on clouds
    with a smile.

In late-night dreams
        you did come back
many times to help me
    peek across the bridge

into your ghostly realities.
    You even returned to lie
in my arms
    with a your soft-feeling fuzz,

        caressing me
        with scented
honey-flowered perfume...
    simply magical!

But it's been so long!
    Why don't you come around
much anymore?
    Have you flown away forever?

I've tried to replace you
    with many others.

But all I sense
    when I look everywhere

are faint whirring hums,
    fetid smells
and the painful
    sting.

A LONELY PEBBLE

The first day
the powerful Sea God
tossed me ashore

into the gloomy blues,
birthing me with bloodied,
salt-watered eyes.

The second day
She sent me Her soft
whispering waves

to cool my heart as if to
show me She was no longer
a maternal stranger.

The third day I dove into
Her to worship—no to beg Her
that I not lose her, too.

The fourth day
I was at the mercy of Wind God
who swept me here and there—

though once I was a large stone—
shrinking me to a pebble.
My anger

soared as I regressed
from my elder years into a tiny
spirit, still tied to him and you.

Why? Because you left me
red-eyed and alone, and now
you're with dead daddy, mom.

SCORCHED INNOCENCE

Looking at you I see black clouds
lanced by lightning

    compressed in the wings
    of a diving swallow,

one who mimics
a falcon's skill to kill.

    You sway on life's stage
    still reaching out,

but your steel-toed slippers
    are out of step with warmth,

and stomp tenderness to a limp
as you mumble off-key

    blues tunes torn
    from a childhood ruined.

Slow dancing with
skeleton shadows, you flash

    a needle-like stare
    that pricks all who probe

your unease. I see,
within you, a girl kneeling

in church and trembling,
face down, out of place,

blood-stained liquid
oozing out around her wrist,

just past a fading Jesus tattoo—
on her trigger finger.

Puzzled, but strangely attracted to you,
I stagger into my imagination and witness

serpents and cold-blooded
alligators roaming around you,

your protectors as you begin to embrace
your afterlife.

I move in close
and hear you praying to be able

to leave this play of life to be freed
of men, even those like me,

who are seduced by your
seeming innocence, then scorched

from your abused-blaze childhood
and mysterious allure.

PONDEROUS PAWS BLUES

I stare
at the lures of the day—

    flimsy clothes
    caressing blossoming bodies, vanished

views of earlier years. Though I try
to stand erect, to execute

    the kinetics of strut,
    like a crack-addicted crab

I crawl sideways, sliding
into dark, dank caverns

    of carnal memories.
    Loss of face measures me

for a fitting of funk
making even Buddha weep

    at the sight of a spirit spent.
    Scalpels of irrelevance

slice my core,
finding it shallow...

surgery too late for an aging
creature crumbled by surface

living. I am a masterpiece creation
of sensually molded mush,

conceived in dawn's light,
then slowly sculpted

into a spirit of obscurity
by the ponderous paws of time.

MOZART DIGS HIP HOP

Pavarotti was ill.
Who stepped up but the Queen

of Soul, Aretha Franklin, to sing,
beautifully, *Nessun dorma.*

Now I can imagine someone, say
Mozart, writing a funky-sweet composition

after falling in love with Rapper Missy Elliot's
Hip Hop *Hot Boyz*, a symphony

that could make butterflies flutter and flirt
with hip-hopping bullfrogs,

Queen Elizabeth tenderly hum
British Blues to B. B. King,

and black ravens softly caw
as they court snow-white doves.

Perhaps all odd pairings
can be linked and transformed,

like Moon, a cold dark rock,
becomes bedazzled and rebirthed

luminous, when paired
with sun's fiery flame.

ANIMAL RELATIONSHIPS

I want you. I shouldn't want
you. I don't want to want
you, but I love wanting.

I want to want someone
who wants me. You want me but you don't
want to? You love wanting too, don't you?

I satisfy you with some of your wants
but you want me to want you
more and want all of me?

No way. I want to want you,
have my wants wanted
and walk away whenever I want.

Can't you want me
without want-chains? Why
do you frown on my wants?

Is it because I want you
to want me solely? Well,
I want to be contradictory,

make no sense and have you
want me anyway and be loved
for the shallow person I am.

Don't you know most selfish
people want to be wanted
by someone? Everyone!

You want me
to want you unconditionally
like a dog, so you can say

won't you lick me whether you
want to or not? What if I try
to be that dog?

So, still you're not sure you want
me? Depends on the kind of dog
you want at the time? Sometimes

you want one to be cuddly and
submissive. At other times you want
a strong, aggressive one who'll protect you,

satisfy all your wants,
wag its tail and sit
on your command!

Noooo, no way!!! I'd rather be a cat,
get in your lap, get stroked,
purrrrr and leave whenever I want.

Well, some nights I want to be
that cat, but I just can't shake the
howl of that wild dog in me.

THE LEASH

I'm your dog.
   You grasp my tail,
wagging me wildly.

I'm also your cat,
   frenzied by the catnip
scents of you.

But what if I were a cat
   on the days you want me
to wag

and doggish on cat days
   oblivious to the pull
of any feline-luring nip?

Then who would be seized
   and in bondage to the leash
of commanding love?

NARCISSIST LEADER'S MANIFESTO

Look at me
    and be mesmerized,
my mindless morons.

I will cure you
    of ignorance and increase
your intelligence

if you promise to be
    in more appropriate awe
of me.

Deep down inside, you
    may know my tricky truths
are a sham, but still

afford me the credit I'm due,
    for I'm beautiful
and a guru at what I do.

Stare in awe!
    One must praise
true artistry involved

in the sleight of hand. Allow
    yourselves to be hypnotized
and paralyzed. Lies aside,

even God has no choice
    but to admire and admit that
I am the model of suave,

a master magician who can
    make truths die in muddied waters.
I deserve well-earned praise.

Submit now and accept only my news
    and join my flummoxed flock.
Or else!

RUSTY REBEL

Comfortable in my pajamas,
I switch channels

from morning news protesting
semi-automatic murders,

death of earth, womb control
and Black Lives Matter

and I blithely move on
to ESPN and MTV—

I no longer feel
the sixties rebel in me.

My pupils open wide
as my self-image tightens

from an Irrelevance Noose
around my neck.

Colors fade. A blue jay's still
on the windowsill,

opened beaked,
with no sound.

I slouch down further
in my soft recliner, unable

to view the scenes of refugee kids
who crawl in alleys of grief.

Somewhere within this rot
that Soul exists.

Just rusty I tell myself,
as I sip stale rum

and sing my part
in the Chorus of the Lost.

FREE SPIRITS ON TREADMILLS

God, I need a switch
of spirit guides! I want one
who has mastered the art

of living on the rim
of reason,
a rascally one

who has been reincarnated
a dozen or so times.
Give me a guide

born in Mongolia,
orphaned at the age of eight,
a runaway raised in the jungle

by blind albino pygmies
before doing a stint
with some liberationist nuns,

and in another life
was a Monk turned
samurai warrior who came out

loud and proud
slashing his blade
for all folks oppressed.

I want a guide with a taste
for Belgian hip-hop and
Norwegian Pentecostal tunes,

one who has not only lived
on the edge but one who also
has an edge,

because I think we are stuck
in the muck fighting
the same old fights

on these rusty treadmills
of lifelessly loving the norm.
And Lord, I could use

a blessed hammer or two
for, with all due respect, if I ever
find the spiritual mechanics

who didn't oil this rusty treadmill,
I'll nail their slothful souls
to the walls of purgatory!

LADYBUG AND APHIDS:
A MURDERERS MUSICAL

Lil Ladybug sporting
   some little-bug earphones
floated on an emerald

   leaf in a sapphire sea.
     She reveled in the briny smells
from summer's breeze, and chilled

     to some soulful Ben Webster jazz.
      She didn't see the ghosts
of aphids she'd eaten sneak on board.

     Under a butter-blue sky, the aphids
       snickered, for you know ghosts can see
the coming of swells and squalls.

     They wanted to witness her
      sink, she, who had swallowed
them whole. But Ladybug switched

   to a new bug music channel and heard
     bluesman Buddy Guy
croon his tune *I Smell Trouble,*

priming Ladybug, just in time,
    to speed the paddling of her wings
on her red and black shell. The aphids,

    startled now, held on. She smirked,
        stretched her wings, paddled with verve
    and rode the rousing waves,

        sunglasses still on straight. Tickled
            by the thrill of it all, she sipped
        sea salt margaritas and rolled up

            a small bug-joint, smiled
                and gifted them
            with some aphid-sized joints

                before they all landed
                    in Tahiti. High on aphid weed,
                the ghosts then remembered

            that they had strong appetites too,
                for they feasted on plants. So, resigned
            to the reality that we all murder

        living life to survive,
            they sat back, sighed,
        and rolled up some larger

and larger ghost-joints
    before everyone began grooving
to some gospel, hallelujah singing

    about death and salvation before slowly
        cuing in to Bobby McFerrin's joyous song,
    Don't Worry Be Happy

POETIC ANIMAL DREAMS

Never, I mean never try
to screw over a tiny yellow turtle
who remembers being accosted

near a river by a ruby red racehorse.
Such are the bizarre, unconscious
constructs my mind comes up with

before I wake up from a dream
and sit down to write a poem.
Accosted? How? What? Whoa! Why a turtle?

Why was that turtle tiny...and yellow?
What's it mean that it's near a river?
A ruby red racehorse? Come on, help me!

That's why I love the challenge
of trying to be a "Confessional" poet.
I can conjure up crazy, creepy, crap,

then forage around, dipping into a bit
of my subconscious absurdity, and
try to decipher its symbolic meanings

consult a thesaurus, and then wait
for metaphors and similes
to house themselves in "correct" forms

that will paint a picture of my nuttiness
as semi-sane. In editing, I try not to trash it all.
It's gotta mean something. Know what I mean?

So play along with me with this
poem and dive deeply into my dream
and help me interpret it.

C'mon, my poets and poetry lovers,
marry your peculiarities to your poetic tools
and finish interpreting my dream with me.

Better still, share your own nighttime
quirky minds and make your sense
with writings that create

poetic beauty out of your best bizarre.
Let your madness be revealing and raw,
one Freud's or Jung's followers

would love to quarrel about
regarding their "undeniable"
interpretations of truth!

RAINDROP SOLILOQUY

I am a drop of rain
in a thunderstorm,
a water bead, running,
stopping, swept sideways
then in circles, hip
and hopping down
to you, a puddle
waiting to engulf me

at the bottom
of the windowsill.
Convinced that I would fall
to you from gravity's pull,
you track all my slip-sliding
moves in the arms
of the fury.

Propelled by the wind, I am
like a liquid abstract painting
lit on a wet canvas
as you confidently whisper,
come, come to me now,
as it is the fate of droplets
to be consumed by puddles.

But I persevere
with a firm belief
that I, a small raindrop,
can exercise my will
to alter life's course by fighting
nature's gravitational powers,
yielding only when I must,

as I cascade down and resist
the winds amidst vibrations
of thunder and lightning.
Then I will hit the bottom   alone

wondering what it means for me
to live life fully.

Is it a short-lived experience
of struggle and winning
a battle to maintain my
raindrop identity,
the way to live
before evaporating?

Or should I join
my fellow dissolved raindrops
in a death of our identity
by living
a longer life
within a puddle?

Who am I?
    What might my
        and your God say?

BLACKBERRIES
AND HOMINY GRITS

As jet wings descended
into southern memories,
  my breathing was slowed

by the drawl of ancestors
who warmly welcomed me home,
  away from New England's

tight smiles, diverting eyes
and frosty ties.
  I arrived near Catfish Creek

and saw morning fog
lift her flannel skirt for bluebirds
  flitting and chirping

amidst sounds of slop-eating
hogs, riotous roosters
  and chuck-clucking hens.

I was able to stroll with
my black feet over red clay
  under old moss trees. I recalled

my elders told me about hands,
blood-drenched from picking
  white cotton, the thorny

red-white rose image
symbolic of bondage
  for Southern Black folks.

My mouth watered for juicy
blackberries and hominy grits, one
  of the few soothing black and white

views of my youth.
Mellower memories, though,
  of southern Sunday mornings

caressed me while sitting
back in Grandma's rocking chair
  on the front porch,

as smiling church elders
passed by, looking
  over to say,

How ya doing this morning?
God be with ya
  and have a nice day ya hear?

These gentle greetings
were often sent amidst
  a scat-singing rain

underneath a bright sun,
a scene Black folks
  say meant

the Devil was beating
his wife behind
  the back doorstep.

Author's Note

I have sincere gratitude for the support of my good friend and MFA Solstice Creative Writing Program alum, Lisa Charnock, who gave me some honest, hard to hear at times, but superb feedback and suggestions on all my poems and other aspects of this publication.

This publication has been a process that has lasted for much longer than I assume she expected, even for working with a first-time publishing poet, so I can't thank enough my publisher, Chryss Yost, of Sungold Editions, for having the patience to hang in and advise me on my poems and for every step of the way for getting this project to come to fruition. Her encouragement and ongoing advice and support were both great learning experiences for me and essential in all ways possible for this project to be completed.

Nathaniel Mayes, Jr. first engaged with poetry through the Cantab Lounge Club in Cambridge, MA, participating in spoken word events and from there he 'crossed over' and joined the poetry writing group, the Bagel Bards. Nat's poetry has been published in the Bagel Bards Anthologies 2, 3, and 11. He was mentored in poetry writing workshops by Laure-Anne Bosslelaar, a founding member of the Solstice MFA Creative Writing Program, and he subsequently enrolled in that program where he studied with Professor Kathleen Aguero. A Georgia native, Nat currently lives in San Rafael, California near his son, two daughters, and his grandchild and, in addition to poetry, he loves music of all genres, particularly Jazz.

www.ingramcontent.com/pod-product-compliance
Lightning Source LLC
Chambersburg PA
CBHW070451130626
46553CB00006B/2354